THE

ABIDE

BIBLE JOURNAL

HEBREWS

Phil Collins, PhD
General Editor

WWW.THOMASNELSON.COM

20 21 22 23 24 25 26 27 /AMC/ 15 14 13 12 11 10 9 8 7 6 5 4 3 2 1

HOW TO USE THIS JOURNAL

The NET Abide Bible Journals provide you with key tools for engaging Scripture. You'll find at the beginning of every Bible book an introduction that highlights the book's enduring message and themes as well as information about the author. Along with Scripture you'll also find prompts or sidebars designed to help you engage passages and deepen your understanding and experience of God's Word.

These prompts include the following:

 Contemplate. Following an ancient spiritual pattern (read, meditate, pray, contemplate), you'll ponder specific passages, take time to experience the Lord's presence, and pray according to what you discover.

 Journal. These sections draw attention to particular themes in the passages or questions the text raises. Each prompt is followed by blank lines on which you can record your thoughts as you focus, reflect on, and engage the Bible passage. Journaling encourages honesty, soul-searching, and openness to God's Word.

 Picture It. This section helps you place yourself within the biblical narrative or passage, imagining the sights, sounds, and smells of the Bible events. You will be no longer just a reader but also a witness, participant, or bystander in the story.

 Praying Scripture. All Scripture-engagement practices lead to speaking to and hearing from God. Conversation with God is essential for developing a deeper relationship with Him. These sidebars show you how to pattern your prayer after particular texts of Scripture.

We invite you to use the prompts provided and the journaling space as you see fit. This is a tool for you to use in deepening your relationship with God. Through the *Abide Bible* prompts, all of which are based on the time-tested methods, our hope is that you will genuinely engage with Scripture. As lives are transformed by God through His Word, we believe the church and the world will be influenced for our good and His glory.

TO THE READER

AN INTRODUCTION TO THE NEW ENGLISH TRANSLATION

"You have been born anew . . . through the
living and enduring word of God."

1 Peter 1:23

The New English Translation (NET) is the newest complete translation of the original biblical languages into English. In 1995 a multi-denominational team of more than twenty-five of the world's foremost biblical scholars gathered around the shared vision of creating an English Bible translation that could overcome old challenges and boldly open the door for new possibilities. The translators completed the first edition in 2001 and incorporated revisions based on scholarly and user feedback in 2003 and 2005. In 2019 a major update reached its final stages. The NET's unique translation process has yielded a beautiful, faithful English Bible for the worldwide church today.

What sets the NET Bible apart from other translations? We encourage you to read the full story of the NET's development and additional details about its translation philosophy at netbible.com/net-bible-preface. But we would like to draw your attention to a few features that commend the NET to all readers of the Word.

TRANSPARENT AND ACCOUNTABLE

Have you ever wished you could look over a Bible translator's shoulder as he or she worked?

Bible translation usually happens behind closed doors—few outside the translation committee see the complex decisions underlying the words that appear in their English Bibles. Fewer still have the opportunity to review and speak into the translators' decisions.

Throughout the NET's translation process, every working draft was made publicly available on the Internet. Bible scholars, ministers, and laypersons from around the world logged millions of review sessions. No other translation is so openly accountable to the worldwide church or has been so thoroughly vetted.

And yet, the ultimate accountability was to the biblical text itself. The NET Bible is neither crowdsourced nor a "translation by consensus." Rather, the NET translators filtered every question and suggestion through the very best insights from biblical linguistics, textual criticism, and their unswerving commitment to following the text wherever it leads. Thus, the NET remains supremely accurate and trustworthy, while also benefiting from extensive review by those who would be reading, studying, and teaching from its pages.

BEYOND THE "READABLE VS. ACCURATE" DIVIDE

The uniquely transparent and accountable translation process of the NET has been crystalized in the most extensive set of Bible translators' notes ever created. More than 60,000 notes highlight every major decision, outline alternative views, and explain difficult or nontraditional renderings. Freely available at netbible.org and in print in the *NET Bible, Full Notes Edition*, these notes help the NET overcome one of the biggest challenges facing any Bible translation: the tension between *accuracy* and *readability*.

If you have spent more than a few minutes researching English versions of the Bible, you have probably encountered a "translation spectrum" —a simple chart with the most wooden-but-precise translations on the far left (representing a "word-for-word" translation approach) and the loosest-but-easiest-to-read translations and paraphrases on the far right (representing a "thought-for-thought" philosophy of translation). Some translations intentionally lean toward one end of the spectrum or the other, embracing the strengths and weaknesses of their chosen approach. Most try to strike a balance between the extremes, weighing accuracy against readability—striving to reflect the grammar of the underlying biblical languages while still achieving acceptable English style.

But the NET moves beyond that old dichotomy. Because of the extensive translators' notes, the NET never has to compromise. Whenever faced with a difficult translation choice, the translators were free to put the strongest option in the main text while documenting the challenge, their thought process, and the solution in the notes.

The benefit to you, the reader? You can be sure that the NET is a translation you can trust—nothing has been lost in translation or obscured by a translator's dilemma. Instead, you are invited to see for yourself, and gain the kind of transparent access to the biblical languages previously only available to scholars.

MINISTRY FIRST

One more reason to love the NET: modern Bible translations are typically copyrighted, posing a challenge for ministries hoping to quote more than a few passages in their Bible study resources, curriculum, or other programming. But the NET is for everyone, with "ministry first" copyright innovations that encourage ministries to quote and share the life-changing message of Scripture as freely as possible. In fact, one of the major motivations behind the creation of the NET was the desire to ensure that ministries had unfettered access to a top-quality modern Bible translation, without needing to embark on a complicated process of securing permissions.

Visit netbible.com/net-bible-copyright to learn more.

TAKE UP AND READ

With its balanced, easy-to-understand English text and a transparent translation process that invites you to see for yourself the richness of the biblical languages, the NET is a Bible you can embrace as your own. Clear, readable, elegant, and accurate, the NET presents Scripture as meaningfully and powerfully today as when these words were first communicated to the people of God.

Our prayer is that the NET will be a fresh and exciting invitation to you—and Bible readers everywhere—to "let the word of Christ dwell in you richly" (Col 3:16).

The Publishers

HEBREWS

Hebrews proclaims the centrality and supremacy of Jesus Christ, as well as the finality of the revelation that Jesus gave through His apostles. This revelation is that Christ is greater than all the angels and all the prophets who have gone before Him. In fact, as God the Son, Jesus is the One through whom the whole world was made and all things are sustained (1:2–3). Jesus is the origin and goal of human history (Rev 22:13). As the very image of the Father and the reflection of the Father's glory, Jesus is the ultimate revelation who fulfills all previous revelations (Rev 1:1–2). The incarnation, obedient life, suffering, sacrificial death, resurrection, and ascension of God's Son are the ultimate self-revelation of God, fulfilling the foreshadowing and promises found throughout the Old Testament.

Among the New Testament books, Hebrews uniquely emphasizes the high priesthood of Jesus. Though His priestly work is implied in other books of the New Testament, nowhere else is He named specifically a priest. The author of Hebrews draws our attention to Jesus' holy, pure, and sinless humanity (7:26). And though He was tempted in every way, He never sinned, so He is a High Priest who can sympathize with our weaknesses (4:15). Therefore we may approach God's throne with confidence to gain the grace we need in all circumstances (4:16).

No other book in the New Testament so fully discusses the relationship between the Old Covenant and the New. The author articulated both the continuity and discontinuity between the two covenants.

INTRODUCTION: GOD HAS SPOKEN FULLY AND FINALLY IN HIS SON

1 After God spoke long ago in various portions and in various ways to our ancestors through the prophets, 2 in these last days he has spoken to us in a son, whom he appointed heir of all things, and through whom he created the world. 3 The Son is the radiance of his glory and the representation of his essence, and he sustains all things by his powerful word, and so when he had accomplished cleansing for sins, *he sat down at the right hand of the Majesty on high.* 4 Thus he became so far better than the angels as he has inherited a name superior to theirs.

THE SON IS SUPERIOR TO ANGELS

5 For to which of the angels did God ever say, "*You are my son! Today I have fathered you*"? And in another place he says, "*I will be his father and he will be my son.*" 6 But when he again brings his firstborn into the world, he says, "*Let all the angels of God worship him!*" 7 And he says of the angels, "*He makes his angels winds and his ministers a flame of fire,*" 8 but of the Son he says,

> "*Your throne, O God, is forever and ever,*
> *and a righteous scepter is the scepter of your kingdom.*
> 9 *You have loved righteousness and hated lawlessness.*
> *So God, your God, has anointed you over your*
> *companions with the oil of rejoicing.*"

10 And,

> "*You founded the earth in the beginning, Lord,*
> *and the heavens are the works of your hands.*
> 11 *They will perish, but you continue.*
> *And they will all grow old like a garment,*
> 12 *and like a robe you will fold them up*
> *and* like a garment *they will be changed,*
> *but you are the same and your years will never run out.*"

13 But to which of the angels has he ever said, "*Sit at my right hand until I make your enemies a footstool for your feet*"? 14 Are they not all ministering spirits, sent out to serve those who will inherit salvation?

PRAYING SCRIPTURE

Hebrews 1:1–4

People who want to know who God is can look at Jesus. He is the exact representation of the Father (v. 3). He is not just a philosophy or a platonic ideal. God came to us in human form. The Word (Logos) became flesh and lived among people (John 1:14).

The author of Hebrews wanted us to surrender to the rightful lordship of Jesus. Christ, equal with the Father, is the final authority and fulfillment of the Old Testament revelations. How will we respond to Him? Search your heart and make sure that you have entrusted Jesus with your whole being. Ask God to show you areas in your life where you are not trusting Jesus. Allow Him to rule over all of you.

WARNING AGAINST DRIFTING AWAY

2 Therefore we must pay closer attention to what we have heard, so that we do not drift away. ²For if the message spoken through angels proved to be so firm that every violation or disobedience received its just penalty, ³how will we escape if we neglect such a great salvation? It was first communicated through the Lord and was confirmed to us by those who heard him, ⁴while God confirmed their witness with signs and wonders and various miracles and gifts of the Holy Spirit distributed according to his will.

EXPOSITION OF PSALM 8: JESUS AND THE DESTINY OF HUMANITY

⁵For he did not put the world to come, about which we are speaking, under the control of angels. ⁶Instead someone testified somewhere:

> *"What is man that you think of him or the*
> *son of man that you care for him?*
> ⁷ *You made him lower than the angels for a little while.*
> *You crowned him with glory and honor.*
> ⁸ *You put all things under his control."*

For when he **put all things under his control**, he left nothing outside of his control. At present we do not yet see **all things under his control**, ⁹but we see Jesus, who was made **lower than the angels for a little while**, now crowned with glory and honor because he suffered death, so that by God's grace he would experience death on behalf of everyone. ¹⁰For it was fitting for him, for whom and through whom all things exist, in bringing many sons to glory, to make the pioneer of their salvation perfect through sufferings. ¹¹For indeed he who makes holy and those being made holy all have the same origin, and so he is not ashamed to call them brothers and sisters, ¹²saying, "*I will proclaim your name to my brothers; in the midst of the assembly I will praise you.*" ¹³Again he says, "I will be confident in him," and again, "*Here I am, with the children God has given me.*" ¹⁴Therefore, since the children share in flesh and blood, he likewise shared in their humanity, so that through death

JOURNAL

Hebrews 2:1–4

REFLECT AND WRITE.

- How prone are you to drifting away from the truths of God's Word that you have learned? What truth has God shown you recently that you need to remember and pay close attention to?

- What is the danger of ignoring God's message of salvation?

- In what ways has God confirmed the truth of His Word to us (see v. 4)?

CONTEMPLATE

Hebrews 2:5–18

READ. Hebrews describes the removal of both shame and sin through Jesus' humble obedience. Read the passage thoughtfully. Consider that Christ's work is to bring you to glory (v. 10) and make you part of His family (v. 11).

MEDITATE. Consider the contrast between the glory Jesus achieved and the humbling He accepted on your behalf. In what area of your life do you need Jesus to identify with your humanity? How might He turn your life to eternal glory?

PRAY. Thank God that you have been adopted into His family because of Christ's work and humility.

CONTEMPLATE. Rest knowing Christ has made you part of the family of God. What privileges does this entail? What responsibilities do you share with the other members of God's family?

he could destroy the one who holds the power of death (that is, the devil), [15] and set free those who were held in slavery all their lives by their fear of death. [16] For surely his concern is not for angels, but he is concerned for Abraham's descendants. [17] Therefore he had to be made like his brothers and sisters in every respect, so that he could become a merciful and faithful high priest in things relating to God, to make atonement for the sins of the people. [18] For since he himself suffered when he was tempted, he is able to help those who are tempted.

JESUS AND MOSES

3 Therefore, holy brothers and sisters, partners in a heavenly calling, take note of Jesus, the apostle and high priest whom we confess, [2] who is faithful to the one who appointed him, as Moses was also in God's house. [3] For he has come to deserve greater glory than Moses, just as the builder of a house deserves greater honor than the house itself! [4] For every house is built by someone, but the builder of all things is God. [5] Now Moses was *faithful in all God's house* as a servant, to testify to the things that would be spoken. [6] But Christ is faithful as a son over God's house. We are of his house, if in fact we hold firmly to our confidence and the hope we take pride in.

EXPOSITION OF PSALM 95: HEARING GOD'S WORD IN FAITH

[7] Therefore, as the Holy Spirit says,

> *"Oh, that today you would listen as he speaks!*
>
> [8] *"Do not harden your hearts as in the rebellion,*
> *in the day of testing in the wilderness.*
>
> [9] *"There your fathers tested me and tried me,*
> *and they saw my works for forty years.*
>
> [10] *"Therefore, I became provoked at that generation*
> *and said, 'Their hearts are always wandering*
> *and they have not known my ways.'*
>
> [11] *"As I swore in my anger, 'They will never enter my rest!'"*

JOURNAL

Hebrews 3:7–19

REFLECT AND WRITE.

- Disobedience caused the Israelites to receive punishment for their rebellion after they had been delivered from Egypt. God had a wonderful place set aside for them, but their sin prevented them from entering (see vv. 16–19). What sin has prevented you from receiving God's blessings? Repent and seek His forgiveness today.

- Ask God to bring to mind someone who needs encouragement to firmly stand in their faith.

¹² See to it, brothers and sisters, that none of you has an evil, unbelieving heart that forsakes the living God. ¹³ But exhort one another each day, as long as it is called "Today," that none of you may become hardened by sin's deception. ¹⁴ For we have become partners with Christ, if in fact we hold our initial confidence firm until the end. ¹⁵ As it says, *"Oh, that today you would listen as he speaks! Do not harden your hearts as in the rebellion."* ¹⁶ For which ones heard and rebelled? Was it not all who came out of Egypt under Moses' leadership? ¹⁷ And against whom was God provoked for forty years? Was it not those who sinned, *whose dead bodies fell in the wilderness?* ¹⁸ And to whom did he swear they would never enter into his rest, except those who were disobedient? ¹⁹ So we see that they could not enter because of unbelief.

GOD'S PROMISED REST

4 Therefore we must be wary that, while the promise of entering his rest remains open, none of you may seem to have come short of it. ² For we had good news proclaimed to us just as they did. But the message they heard did them no good, since they did not join in with those who heard it in faith. ³ For we who have believed enter that rest, as he has said, *"As I swore in my anger, 'They will never enter my rest!'"* And yet God's works were accomplished from the foundation of the world. ⁴ For he has spoken somewhere about the seventh day in this way: *"And God rested on the seventh day from all his works,"* ⁵ but to repeat the text cited earlier: *"They will never enter my rest!"* ⁶ Therefore it remains for some to enter it, yet those to whom it was previously proclaimed did not enter because of disobedience. ⁷ So God again ordains a certain day, "Today," speaking through David after so long a time, as in the words quoted before, *"Oh, that today you would listen as he speaks! Do not harden your hearts."* ⁸ For if Joshua had given them rest, God would not have spoken afterward about another day. ⁹ Consequently a Sabbath rest remains for the people of God. ¹⁰ For the one who enters God's rest has also rested from his works, just as God did from his own works. ¹¹ Thus we must make every effort to enter that rest, so that

CONTEMPLATE

Hebrews 4:1–11

READ. Read the passage out loud. Write out any phrase that catches your attention. Circle or underline key words that seem significant to you.

MEDITATE. How do these words relate to the strong warnings in the passage? Take a moment for any necessary self-reflection. Will you, through the obedience of your faith, enter the promised rest (vv. 6–9)?

PRAY. Once you have connected Hebrews 4 to your life, turn that connection into a prayer. Ask God to soften your hard heart and grant you the strength to be diligent in obeying His will. Thank Him for the promise of rest and fellowship with Him.

CONTEMPLATE. Cease from striving and doubt, and faithfully follow God's guidance. Hold fast to His daily care and supervision while you walk with Him.

no one may fall by following the same pattern of disobedience. [12] For the word of God is living and active and sharper than any double-edged sword, piercing even to the point of dividing soul from spirit, and joints from marrow; it is able to judge the desires and thoughts of the heart. [13] And no creature is hidden from God, but everything is naked and exposed to the eyes of him to whom we must render an account.

JESUS OUR COMPASSIONATE HIGH PRIEST

[14] Therefore since we have a great high priest who has passed through the heavens, Jesus the Son of God, let us hold fast to our confession. [15] For we do not have a high priest incapable of sympathizing with our weaknesses, but one who has been tempted in every way just as we are, yet without sin. [16] Therefore let us confidently approach the throne of grace to receive mercy and find grace whenever we need help.

5 For every high priest is taken from among the people and appointed to represent them before God, to offer both gifts and sacrifices for sins. [2] He is able to deal compassionately with those who are ignorant and erring, since he also is subject to weakness, [3] and for this reason he is obligated to make sin offerings for himself as well as for the people. [4] And no one assumes this honor on his own initiative, but only when called to it by God, as in fact Aaron was. [5] So also Christ did not glorify himself in becoming high priest, but the one who glorified him was God, who said to him, "*You are my Son! Today I have fathered you*," [6] as also in another place God says, "*You are a priest forever in the order of Melchizedek*." [7] During his earthly life Christ offered both requests and supplications, with loud cries and tears, to the one who was able to save him from death and he was heard because of his devotion. [8] Although he was a son, he learned obedience through the things he suffered. [9] And by being perfected in this way, he became the source of eternal salvation to all who obey him, [10] and he was designated by God as high priest *in the order of Melchizedek*.

PRAYING SCRIPTURE

Hebrews 4:12–16

The Scriptures have a way of penetrating the soul, seeing our thoughts and attitudes. Nothing is hidden from God, but His Word exposes who we are. For that reason, as we approach His Word, we find every pretense and subterfuge stripped away. Yet we can confidently subject ourselves to this scrutiny because we have a High Priest who sympathizes with us in our humanity. At His throne we find all we need.

As you pray, ask God boldly for the grace and mercy you need.

PICTURE IT

Hebrews 4:14–16

PICTURE. Hebrews systematically describes the superiority of Christ to the old ways of works and sacrifice. Imagine you are seeking an audience with the holy King. You are terrified. All eyes are on you as you enter the forbidden inner place. Suddenly you realize that your brother Christ is there in the room, able to speak to God on your behalf. You may boldly go forward because the One who knows God knows you. By boldly entering you find the grace and mercy necessary to live your mission and life for Christ!

PRAY. Ask for the courage and confidence to approach God Himself, knowing that His Son has already spoken on your behalf.

THE NEED TO MOVE ON TO MATURITY

¹¹ On this topic we have much to say and it is difficult to explain, since you have become sluggish in hearing. ¹² For though you should in fact be teachers by this time, you need someone to teach you the beginning elements of God's utterances. You have gone back to needing milk, not solid food. ¹³ For everyone who lives on milk is inexperienced in the message of righteousness, because he is an infant. ¹⁴ But solid food is for the mature, whose perceptions are trained by practice to discern both good and evil.

6 Therefore we must progress beyond the elementary instructions about Christ and move on to maturity, not laying this foundation again: repentance from dead works and faith in God, ² teaching about ritual washings, laying on of hands, resurrection of the dead, and eternal judgment. ³ And this is what we intend to do, if God permits. ⁴ For it is impossible in the case of those who have once been enlightened, tasted the heavenly gift, become partakers of the Holy Spirit, ⁵ tasted the good word of God and the miracles of the coming age, ⁶ and then have committed apostasy, to renew them again to repentance, since they are crucifying the Son of God for themselves all over again and holding him up to contempt. ⁷ For the ground that has soaked up the rain that frequently falls on it and yields useful vegetation for those who tend it receives a blessing from God. ⁸ But if it produces thorns and thistles, it is useless and about to be cursed; its fate is to be burned. ⁹ But in your case, dear friends, even though we speak like this, we are convinced of better things relating to salvation. ¹⁰ For God is not unjust so as to forget your work and the love you have demonstrated for his name, in having served and continuing to serve the saints. ¹¹ But we passionately want each of you to demonstrate the same eagerness for the fulfillment of your hope until the end, ¹² so that you may not be sluggish, but imitators of those who through faith and perseverance inherit the promises.

¹³ Now when God made his promise to Abraham, since he could swear by no one greater, he swore by himself, ¹⁴ saying, *"Surely I will bless you greatly and multiply your descendants*

JOURNAL

Hebrews 6:4–12

REFLECT AND WRITE.

- What do you remember about your first taste of God's gift of eternal life? What did you think and feel? How have you grown in your faith since that time?

- The author of Hebrews warned his readers not to "be sluggish" in their faith (v. 12). How do we sometimes allow apathy or sluggishness to creep into our spiritual lives? How can you eagerly and patiently work each day to love people as an expression of your faith (see vv. 10–11)?

PRAYING SCRIPTURE

Hebrews 6:13–20

The guarantee of salvation is sure. It has been established by Christ's high priesthood. God was willing to give assurances based on His character and His oath. Give praise to Him for His promises, the encouragement of faith, and His being a refuge for us (vv. 17–18). Life is often tumultuous and threatening, which can cause us to doubt. Thank God that your faith is grounded in truth that anchors you (v. 19). Jesus is our Forerunner, going before God to provide for salvation. Thank God for His Son (v. 20).

abundantly." 15 And so by persevering, Abraham inherited the promise. 16 For people swear by something greater than themselves, and the oath serves as a confirmation to end all dispute. 17 In the same way God wanted to demonstrate more clearly to the heirs of the promise that his purpose was unchangeable, and so he intervened with an oath, 18 so that we who have found refuge in him may find strong encouragement to hold fast to the hope set before us through two unchangeable things, since it is impossible for God to lie. 19 We have this hope as an anchor for the soul, sure and steadfast, which reaches inside behind the curtain, 20 where Jesus our forerunner entered on our behalf, since he became *a priest forever in the order of Melchizedek.*

THE NATURE OF MELCHIZEDEK'S PRIESTHOOD

7 Now this *Melchizedek, king of Salem, priest of the most high God, met Abraham as he was returning from defeating the kings* and *blessed him.* 2 To him also *Abraham apportioned a tithe of everything.* His name first means king of righteousness, then *king of Salem,* that is, king of peace. 3 Without father, without mother, without genealogy, he has neither beginning of days nor end of life but is like the son of God, and he remains a priest for all time. 4 But see how great he must be, if Abraham the patriarch gave him a tithe of his plunder. 5 And those of the sons of Levi who receive the priestly office have authorization according to the law to collect a tithe from the people, that is, from their fellow countrymen, although they too are descendants of Abraham. 6 But Melchizedek who does not share their ancestry collected a tithe from Abraham and blessed the one who possessed the promise. 7 Now without dispute the inferior is blessed by the superior, 8 and in one case tithes are received by mortal men, while in the other by him who is affirmed to be alive. 9 And it could be said that Levi himself, who receives tithes, paid a tithe through Abraham. 10 For he was still in his ancestor Abraham's loins when Melchizedek met him.

JOURNAL

Hebrews 7:1–7

REFLECT AND WRITE.

- Who was Melchizedek? How is he compared to Jesus (see v. 3)? How is Jesus our High Priest (see Heb 7:26; 9:11–15)?

- What did Abraham give Melchizedek (see vv. 2, 4)? What does this show you about this king's status? How might that point to Jesus, an even greater King?

JESUS AND THE PRIESTHOOD OF MELCHIZEDEK

[11] So if perfection had in fact been possible through the Levitical priesthood—for on that basis the people received the law—what further need would there have been for another priest to arise, said to be in the order of Melchizedek and not in Aaron's order? [12] For when the priesthood changes, a change in the law must come as well. [13] Yet the one these things are spoken about belongs to a different tribe, and no one from that tribe has ever officiated at the altar. [14] For it is clear that our Lord is descended from Judah, yet Moses said nothing about priests in connection with that tribe. [15] And this is even clearer if another priest arises in the likeness of Melchizedek, [16] who has become a priest not by a legal regulation about physical descent but by the power of an indestructible life. [17] For here is the testimony about him: "*You are a priest forever in the order of Melchizedek.*" [18] On the one hand a former command is set aside because it is weak and useless, [19] for the law made nothing perfect. On the other hand a better hope is introduced, through which we draw near to God. [20] And since this was not done without a sworn affirmation—for the others have become priests without a sworn affirmation, [21] but Jesus did so with a sworn affirmation by the one who said to him, "*The Lord has sworn and will not change his mind, 'You are a priest forever'*"—[22] accordingly Jesus has become the guarantee of a better covenant. [23] And the others who became priests were numerous, because death prevented them from continuing in office, [24] but he holds his priesthood permanently since he lives forever. [25] So he is able to save completely those who come to God through him, because he always lives to intercede for them. [26] For it is indeed fitting for us to have such a high priest: holy, innocent, undefiled, separate from sinners, and exalted above the heavens. [27] He has no need to do every day what those priests do, to offer sacrifices first for their own sins and then for the sins of the people, since he did this in offering himself once for all. [28] For the law appoints as high priests men subject to weakness, but the word of solemn affirmation that came after the law appoints a son made perfect forever.

CONTEMPLATE

Hebrews 7:18–28

READ. Read these verses that discuss the utmost effectiveness of Christ as the final and eternal High Priest. Take note of any word, phrase, or verse that catches your attention. Note especially the contrasts to the Levitical priesthood.

MEDITATE. Which fulfillment of Christ's priesthood draws your attention? Why does this aspect seem particularly important to you? Spend time considering His superior qualities. Reflect on the truth that Christ is the permanent High Priest who offered Himself on your behalf.

PRAY. Once you have reflected on what it means for Christ to be your perfect High Priest, bring Him an offering of praise and gratitude.

CONTEMPLATE. Rest in the perfect, finished work of Christ, who always lives to intercede for us before the Father (v. 25).

THE HIGH PRIEST OF A BETTER COVENANT

8 Now the main point of what we are saying is this: We have such a high priest, one who *sat down at the right hand of the throne of the Majesty in heaven,* ² a minister in the sanctuary and the true tabernacle that the Lord, not man, set up. ³ For every high priest is appointed to offer both gifts and sacrifices. So this one too had to have something to offer. ⁴ Now if he were on earth, he would not be a priest, since there are already priests who offer the gifts prescribed by the law. ⁵ The place where they serve is a sketch and shadow of the heavenly sanctuary, just as Moses was warned by God as he was about to complete the tabernacle. For he says, "***See that you make everything according to the design shown to you on the mountain.***" ⁶ But now Jesus has obtained a superior ministry, since the covenant that he mediates is also better and is enacted on better promises.

⁷ For if that first covenant had been faultless, no one would have looked for a second one. ⁸ But showing its fault, God says to them,

> *"Look, the days are coming, says the Lord, when*
> *I will complete a new covenant with the house*
> *of Israel and with the house of Judah.*
>
> ⁹ *"It will not be like the covenant that I made with*
> *their fathers, on the day when I took them by*
> *the hand to lead them out of Egypt, because*
> *they did not continue in my covenant and I*
> *had no regard for them, says the Lord.*
>
> ¹⁰ *"For this is the covenant that I will establish with*
> *the house of Israel after those days, says the*
> *Lord. I will put my laws in their minds and I*
> *will inscribe them on their hearts. And I will*
> *be their God and they will be my people.*
>
> ¹¹ *"And there will be no need at all for each one to*
> *teach his countryman or each one to teach his*
> *brother saying, 'Know the Lord,' since they will*
> *all know me, from the least to the greatest.*
>
> ¹² *"For I will be merciful toward their evil deeds,*
> *and their sins I will remember no longer."*

PRAYING
SCRIPTURE

Hebrews 8:1–12

Jesus provides forgiveness to His people. Because of His perfect obedience and sacrifice, the promises of the New Covenant are realized and are now written onto the hearts and minds of God's people. As you read, take special note of the outcome of Christ's superior priesthood. As you pray, praise Christ for being the perfect Intermediary who established the New Covenant (v. 10) and fulfilled its promises (v. 6). Ask God to reveal Himself to your neighbors and throughout your community (v. 11). Thank God that Jesus' sacrifice permanently removes sin and guilt and that the Father no longer holds our sins against us (v. 12).

¹³When he speaks of a new covenant, he makes the first obsolete. Now what is growing obsolete and aging is about to disappear.

THE ARRANGEMENT AND RITUAL
OF THE EARTHLY SANCTUARY

9 Now the first covenant, in fact, had regulations for worship and its earthly sanctuary. ²For a tent was prepared, the outer one, which contained the lampstand, the table, and the presentation of the loaves; this is called the Holy Place. ³And after the second curtain there was a tent called the holy of holies. ⁴It contained the golden altar of incense and the ark of the covenant covered entirely with gold. In this ark were the golden urn containing the manna, Aaron's rod that budded, and the stone tablets of the covenant. ⁵And above the ark were the cherubim of glory overshadowing the mercy seat. Now is not the time to speak of these things in detail. ⁶So with these things prepared like this, the priests enter continually into the outer tent as they perform their duties. ⁷But only the high priest enters once a year into the inner tent, and not without blood that he offers for himself and for the sins of the people committed in ignorance. ⁸The Holy Spirit is making clear that the way into the Holy Place had not yet appeared as long as the old tabernacle was standing. ⁹This was a symbol for the time then present, when gifts and sacrifices were offered that could not perfect the conscience of the worshiper. ¹⁰They served only for matters of food and drink and various ritual washings; they are external regulations imposed until the new order came.

CHRIST'S SERVICE IN THE
HEAVENLY SANCTUARY

¹¹But now Christ has come as the high priest of the good things to come. He passed through the greater and more perfect tent not made with hands, that is, not of this creation, ¹²and he entered once for all into the Most Holy Place not by the blood of goats and calves but by his own blood, and so he himself secured eternal redemption. ¹³For if the blood

JOURNAL

Hebrews 9:11–28

REFLECT AND WRITE.

- If you have received salvation through Jesus, then your sins are completely forgiven. How does that make you feel (see vv. 11–14)?

- Your conscience has been freed from slavery to dead works and you can serve God in true freedom. What will you do to celebrate your freedom to serve Him (see vv. 13–14)?

- Christ, your Intermediary, permanently pleads your case before God (see v. 24). How is Christ's role as Mediator similar to the role of an Old Testament priest? Thank Jesus for standing before God on your behalf.

of goats and bulls and the ashes of a young cow sprinkled on those who are defiled consecrated them and provided ritual purity, ¹⁴ how much more will the blood of Christ, who through the eternal Spirit offered himself without blemish to God, purify our consciences from dead works to worship the living God.

¹⁵ And so he is the mediator of a new covenant, so that those who are called may receive the eternal inheritance he has promised, since he died to set them free from the violations committed under the first covenant. ¹⁶ For where there is a will, the death of the one who made it must be proven. ¹⁷ For a will takes effect only at death, since it carries no force while the one who made it is alive. ¹⁸ So even the first covenant was inaugurated with blood. ¹⁹ For when Moses had spoken every command to all the people according to the law, he took the blood of calves and goats with water and scarlet wool and hyssop and sprinkled both the book itself and all the people, ²⁰ and said, "*This is the blood of the covenant that God has commanded you to keep.*" ²¹ And both the tabernacle and all the utensils of worship he likewise sprinkled with blood. ²² Indeed according to the law almost everything was purified with blood, and without the shedding of blood there is no forgiveness. ²³ So it was necessary for the sketches of the things in heaven to be purified with these sacrifices, but the heavenly things themselves required better sacrifices than these. ²⁴ For Christ did not enter a sanctuary made with hands—the representation of the true sanctuary—but into heaven itself, and he appears now in God's presence for us. ²⁵ And he did not enter to offer himself again and again, the way the high priest enters the sanctuary year after year with blood that is not his own, ²⁶ for then he would have had to suffer again and again since the foundation of the world. But now he has appeared once for all at the consummation of the ages to put away sin by his sacrifice. ²⁷ And just as people are appointed to die once, and then to face judgment, ²⁸ so also, after Christ was offered once to *bear the sins of many*, to those who eagerly await him he will appear a second time, not to bear sin but to bring salvation.

CONCLUDING EXPOSITION: OLD AND NEW SACRIFICES CONTRASTED

10 For the law possesses a shadow of the good things to come but not the reality itself, and is therefore completely unable, by the same sacrifices offered continually, year after year, to perfect those who come to worship. ² For otherwise would they not have ceased to be offered, since the worshipers would have been purified once for all and so have no further consciousness of sin? ³ But in those sacrifices there is a reminder of sins year after year. ⁴ For it is impossible for the blood of bulls and goats to take away sins. ⁵ So when he came into the world, he said,

> *"Sacrifice and offering you did not desire,*
> *but a body you prepared for me.*
> 6 *"Whole burnt offerings and sin-offerings*
> *you took no delight in.*
> 7 *"Then I said, 'Here I am: I have come—it is written of me*
> *in the scroll of the book—to do your will, O God.'"*

⁸ When he says above, *"Sacrifices and offerings* and *whole burnt offerings and sin-offerings you did not desire nor did you take delight* in them"* (which are offered according to the law), ⁹ then he says, *"Here I am: I have come to do your will."* He does away with the first to establish the second. ¹⁰ By his will we have been made holy through the offering of the body of Jesus Christ once for all. ¹¹ And every priest stands day after day serving and offering the same sacrifices again and again—sacrifices that can never take away sins. ¹² But when this priest had offered one sacrifice for sins for all time, *he sat down at the right hand* of God, ¹³ where he is now waiting *until his enemies are made a footstool for his feet.* ¹⁴ For by one offering he has perfected for all time those who are made holy. ¹⁵ And the Holy Spirit also witnesses to us, for after saying, ¹⁶ *"This is the covenant that I will establish with them after those days, says the Lord. I will put my laws on their hearts and I will inscribe them on their minds,"* ¹⁷ then he says, *"Their sins and their lawless deeds I will remember no longer."* ¹⁸ Now where there is forgiveness of these, there is no longer any offering for sin.

CONTEMPLATE

Hebrews 10:1–14

READ. Read through the passage twice. Reflect on what you know about the requirements of the Old Testament sacrifices. Allow the Spirit to highlight a word, phrase, or verse for you. Consider "a body you prepared for me" (v. 5) or "Here I am: I have come . . . to do your will" (v. 7).

MEDITATE. Christ's sacrifice fulfilled every righteous requirement of the Law. Striving, feelings of inadequacy, and guilt can be handed over to Christ in exchange for His mind and His ways. Consider how you become more like Christ the more you spend time with Him.

PRAY. Turn your meditations from these verses into prayer. Make sure to include gratitude for Christ's willingness to do the will of the Father.

CONTEMPLATE. Rest a moment and take time to remember the joy of your salvation.

DRAWING NEAR TO GOD IN ENDURING FAITH

¹⁹ Therefore, brothers and sisters, since we have confidence to enter the sanctuary by the blood of Jesus, ²⁰ by the fresh and living way that he inaugurated for us through the curtain, that is, through his flesh, ²¹ and since we have a great priest over the house of God, ²² let us draw near with a sincere heart in the assurance that faith brings, because we have had our hearts sprinkled clean from an evil conscience and our bodies washed in pure water. ²³ And let us hold unwaveringly to the hope that we confess, for the one who made the promise is trustworthy. ²⁴ And let us take thought of how to spur one another on to love and good works, ²⁵ not abandoning our own meetings, as some are in the habit of doing, but encouraging each other, and even more so because you see the day drawing near.

²⁶ For if we deliberately keep on sinning after receiving the knowledge of the truth, no further sacrifice for sins is left for us, ²⁷ but only a certain fearful expectation of judgment and *a fury of fire that will consume God's enemies.* ²⁸ Someone who rejected the law of Moses was put to death without mercy *on the testimony of two or three witnesses.* ²⁹ How much greater punishment do you think that person deserves who has contempt for the Son of God, and profanes the blood of the covenant that made him holy, and insults the Spirit of grace? ³⁰ For we know the one who said, "***Vengeance is mine, I will repay,***" and again, "***The Lord will judge his people.***" ³¹ It is a terrifying thing to fall into the hands of the living God.

³² But remember the former days when you endured a harsh conflict of suffering after you were enlightened. ³³ At times you were publicly exposed to abuse and afflictions, and at other times you came to share with others who were treated in that way. ³⁴ For in fact you shared the sufferings of those in prison, and you accepted the confiscation of your belongings with joy, because you knew that you certainly had a better and lasting possession. ³⁵ So do not throw away your confidence, because it has great reward. ³⁶ For you need endurance in order to do God's will and so receive what is promised. ³⁷ For ***just a little longer*** and ***he who is coming will arrive***

CONTEMPLATE

Hebrews 10:19–25

READ. As you read the passage, pay careful attention to the necessary response to our great salvation.

MEDITATE. You are called to approach God with confidence (v. 19), to hold to the hope you confess (v. 23), and to encourage other believers (v. 24). How does your hope in Christ motivate you in these three areas?

PRAY. The exhortation in this passage can be made into a prayer. Rephrase the commands into requests to God. Ask that you would boldly approach the throne, encourage the faith of others, and hold unwaveringly to the hope you confess.

CONTEMPLATE. The author of Hebrews mentions "the day drawing near" (v. 25). How does God encourage believers to persevere until then?

 PRAYING SCRIPTURE

Hebrews 10:32–39

These verses in Hebrews recall how the readers endured suffering (vv. 32–34) without losing hope. The writer called them to live courageously by faith. Reflect on the many instances throughout the Bible in which God demonstrated His faithfulness, provision, and strength to those in need. Ask God to give you that firm faith. Pray that God would help you encourage a friend or relative who is enduring suffering or wavering in their faith. Pray that God would give endurance to all His followers.

and not delay. 38 *But my righteous one will live by faith, and if he shrinks back, I take no pleasure in him.* 39 But we are not among those who shrink back and thus perish, but are among those who have faith and preserve their souls.

PEOPLE COMMENDED FOR THEIR FAITH

11 Now faith is being sure of what we hope for, being convinced of what we do not see. 2 For by it the people of old received God's commendation. 3 By faith we understand that the worlds were set in order at God's command, so that the visible has its origin in the invisible. 4 By faith Abel offered God a greater sacrifice than Cain, and through his faith he was commended as righteous, because God commended him for his offerings. And through his faith he still speaks, though he is dead. 5 By faith Enoch was taken up so that he did not see death, and he was not to be found because God took him up. For before his removal he had been commended as having pleased God. 6 Now without faith it is impossible to please him, for the one who approaches God must believe that he exists and that he rewards those who seek him. 7 By faith Noah, when he was warned about things not yet seen, with reverent regard constructed an ark for the deliverance of his family. Through faith he condemned the world and became an heir of the righteousness that comes by faith.

8 By faith Abraham obeyed when he was called to go out to a place he would later receive as an inheritance, and he went out without understanding where he was going. 9 By faith he lived as a foreigner in the promised land as though it were a foreign country, living in tents with Isaac and Jacob, who were fellow heirs of the same promise. 10 For he was looking forward to the city with firm foundations, whose architect and builder is God. 11 By faith, even though Sarah herself was barren and he was too old, he received the ability to procreate, because he regarded the one who had given the promise to be trustworthy. 12 So in fact children were fathered by one man—and this one as good as dead—*like the number of stars in the sky and like the innumerable grains of sand on the seashore.* 13 These all died in faith without receiving the things

JOURNAL

Hebrews 11:1–40

REFLECT AND WRITE.

- The writer of Hebrews repeated the words *by faith* to describe several believers from the past (vv. 4–12). What example do these people give you in how to lead your life?

- God made promises to these people that were not revealed in their lifetimes. How are these faithful people examples of waiting with patience? What gave them the ability to persevere?

promised, but they saw them in the distance and welcomed them and acknowledged that they were strangers and foreigners on the earth. ¹⁴ For those who speak in such a way make it clear that they are seeking a homeland. ¹⁵ In fact, if they had been thinking of the land that they had left, they would have had opportunity to return. ¹⁶ But as it is, they aspire to a better land, that is, a heavenly one. Therefore, God is not ashamed to be called their God, for he has prepared a city for them. ¹⁷ By faith Abraham, when he was tested, offered up Isaac. He had received the promises, yet he was ready to offer up his only son. ¹⁸ God had told him, *"Through Isaac descendants will carry on your name,"* ¹⁹ and he reasoned that God could even raise him from the dead, and in a sense he received him back from there. ²⁰ By faith also Isaac blessed Jacob and Esau concerning the future. ²¹ By faith Jacob, as he was dying, blessed each of the sons of Joseph and **worshiped as he leaned on his staff.** ²² By faith Joseph, at the end of his life, mentioned the exodus of the sons of Israel and gave instructions about his burial.

²³ By faith, when Moses was born, his parents hid him for three months, because they saw the child was beautiful and they were not afraid of the king's edict. ²⁴ By faith, when he grew up, Moses refused to be called the son of Pharaoh's daughter, ²⁵ choosing rather to be ill-treated with the people of God than to enjoy sin's fleeting pleasure. ²⁶ He regarded abuse suffered for Christ to be greater wealth than the treasures of Egypt, for his eyes were fixed on the reward. ²⁷ By faith he left Egypt without fearing the king's anger, for he persevered as though he could see the one who is invisible. ²⁸ By faith he kept the Passover and the sprinkling of the blood, so that the one who destroyed the firstborn would not touch them. ²⁹ By faith they crossed the Red Sea as if on dry ground, but when the Egyptians tried it, they were swallowed up. ³⁰ By faith the walls of Jericho fell after the people marched around them for seven days. ³¹ By faith Rahab the prostitute escaped the destruction of the disobedient, because she welcomed the spies in peace.

³² And what more shall I say? For time will fail me if I tell of Gideon, Barak, Samson, Jephthah, of David and Samuel and the prophets. ³³ Through faith they conquered kingdoms, administered justice, gained what was promised, shut the mouths of lions, ³⁴ quenched raging fire, escaped the edge of the sword, gained strength in weakness, became mighty in battle, put foreign armies to flight, ³⁵ and women received back their dead raised to life. But others were tortured, not accepting release, to obtain resurrection to a better life. ³⁶ And others experienced mocking and flogging, and even chains and imprisonment. ³⁷ They were stoned, sawed apart, murdered with the sword; they went about in sheepskins and goatskins; they were destitute, afflicted, ill-treated ³⁸ (the world was not worthy of them); they wandered in deserts and mountains and caves and openings in the earth. ³⁹ And these all were commended for their faith, yet they did not receive what was promised. ⁴⁰ For God had provided something better for us, so that they would be made perfect together with us.

THE LORD'S DISCIPLINE

12 Therefore, since we are surrounded by such a great cloud of witnesses, we must get rid of every weight and the sin that clings so closely, and run with endurance the race set out for us, ² keeping our eyes fixed on Jesus, the pioneer and perfecter of our faith. For the joy set out for him he endured the cross, disregarding its shame, and *has taken his seat at the right hand of the throne* of God. ³ Think of him who endured such opposition against himself by sinners, so that you may not grow weary in your souls and give up. ⁴ You have not yet resisted to the point of bloodshed in your struggle against sin. ⁵ And have you forgotten the exhortation addressed to you as sons?

"My son, do not scorn the Lord's discipline
or give up when he corrects you.
⁶ *"For the Lord disciplines the one he loves*
and chastises every son he accepts."

PICTURE IT

Hebrews 12:1–3

PICTURE. In this text the author invites you to hear the roar and see the throngs lining the race. Each face is a hero of the faith. They expectantly watch as you run your course and use their example as an encouragement to persevere. You look down and see you are entangled. Sin ensnares you and threatens to trip you up. Fatigue and doubt set in, sapping your strength and endurance. Your eyes are directed to a figure who once carried the burden of a cross. He is seated at God's right hand, beckoning you to follow Him and finish the race.

PRAY. Verse 3 instructs you to consider Jesus in order to prevent faintness or weariness. Pray that Jesus would be your vision, encourager, and your finish line as you persevere.

PRAYING SCRIPTURE

Hebrews 12:5–11

Discipline is a sign of God's love. Think of it this way: if a coach doesn't train the player, it means the coach doesn't care about the player. Training isn't always pleasant, but it teaches athletes to learn from their mistakes and achieve their best.

Likewise, God's character training is to be received with gratitude because we know it brings wisdom and righteousness. Hebrews exhorts us to endure chastening with patience, as children endure discipline from their parents (v. 7). Ask God for endurance so you may grow in the righteousness and wisdom that will help you defeat sin.

7 Endure your suffering as discipline; God is treating you as sons. For what son is there that a father does not discipline? 8 But if you do not experience discipline, something all sons have shared in, then you are illegitimate and are not sons. 9 Besides, we have experienced discipline from our earthly fathers and we respected them; shall we not submit ourselves all the more to the Father of spirits and receive life? 10 For they disciplined us for a little while as seemed good to them, but he does so for our benefit, that we may share his holiness. 11 Now all discipline seems painful at the time, not joyful. But later it produces the fruit of peace and righteousness for those trained by it. 12 Therefore, **strengthen your listless hands and your weak knees**, 13 and **make straight paths for your feet**, so that what is lame may not be put out of joint but be healed.

DO NOT REJECT GOD'S WARNING

14 Pursue peace with everyone, and holiness, for without it no one will see the Lord. 15 See to it that no one comes short of the grace of God, that no one be like *a bitter root springing up* and causing trouble, and through it many become defiled. 16 And see to it that no one becomes an immoral or godless person like Esau, who *sold his own birthright for a single meal*. 17 For you know that later when he wanted to inherit the blessing, he was rejected, for he found no opportunity for repentance, although he sought the blessing with tears. 18 For you have not come to something that can be touched, to a burning fire and darkness and gloom and a whirlwind 19 and the blast of a trumpet and a voice uttering words such that those who heard begged to hear no more. 20 For they could not bear what was commanded: "*If even an animal touches the mountain, it must be stoned.*" 21 In fact, the scene was so terrifying that Moses said, "*I shudder with fear.*" 22 But you have come to Mount Zion, the city of the living God, the heavenly Jerusalem, and to myriads of angels, to the assembly 23 and congregation of the firstborn, who are enrolled in heaven, and to God, the judge of all, and to the spirits of the righteous, who have been made perfect, 24 and to Jesus, the mediator

JOURNAL

Hebrews 12:18–29

REFLECT AND WRITE.

- In what ways are you looking forward to living forever in the presence of Jesus (see vv. 22–24)?

- How is Jesus the "mediator of a new covenant" (v. 24)? What consequence awaits those who reject Him?

- God has promised Jesus' followers a place in His unshakable kingdom. How will you offer acceptable worship to Him today in response to that promise?

of a new covenant, and to the sprinkled blood that speaks of something better than Abel's does.

²⁵ Take care not to refuse the one who is speaking! For if they did not escape when they refused the one who warned them on earth, how much less shall we, if we reject the one who warns from heaven? ²⁶ Then his voice shook the earth, but now he has promised, *"I will once more shake not only the earth but heaven too."* ²⁷ Now this phrase *"once more"* indicates the removal of what is shaken, that is, of created things, so that what is unshaken may remain. ²⁸ So since we are receiving an unshakable kingdom, let us give thanks, and through this let us offer worship pleasing to God in devotion and awe. ²⁹ For our *God is indeed a devouring fire.*

FINAL EXHORTATIONS

13 Brotherly love must continue. ² Do not neglect hospitality, because through it some have entertained angels without knowing it. ³ Remember those in prison as though you were in prison with them, and those ill-treated as though you too felt their torment. ⁴ Marriage must be honored among all and the marriage bed kept undefiled, for God will judge sexually immoral people and adulterers. ⁵ Your conduct must be free from the love of money and you must be content with what you have, for he has said, *"I will never leave you and I will never abandon you."* ⁶ So we can say with confidence, *"The Lord is my helper, and I will not be afraid. What can people do to me?"* ⁷ Remember your leaders, who spoke God's message to you; reflect on the outcome of their lives and imitate their faith. ⁸ Jesus Christ is the same yesterday and today and forever! ⁹ Do not be carried away by all sorts of strange teachings. For it is good for the heart to be strengthened by grace, not ritual meals, which have never benefited those who participated in them. ¹⁰ We have an altar that those who serve in the tabernacle have no right to eat from. ¹¹ For the bodies of those animals whose blood the high priest brings into the sanctuary as an offering for sin are burned outside the camp. ¹² Therefore, to sanctify the people by his own blood, Jesus also suffered outside the camp. ¹³ We must go out to him, then,

CONTEMPLATE

Hebrews 13:1–18

READ. This chapter concludes Hebrews with specific moral exhortations that follow the previous chapters describing Christ's fulfillment of the Law. As you read the verses, ask the Spirit to highlight one of these concluding commands for meditation.

MEDITATE. Which command stood out to you? Why might the Spirit call your attention to this specific area? What would it look like to act on this command? What will be your sacrifice of obedience?

PRAY. Take your revelations to God in prayer. Thank Him for illuminating His Word, and practice the sacrifice of praise in verse 15.

CONTEMPLATE. After your offering of praise, know that God is pleased with what you have brought Him in obedience (v. 16). Let it become your practice to continually offer Him the fruit of your lips.

outside the camp, bearing the abuse he experienced. [14] For here we have no lasting city, but we seek the city that is to come. [15] Through him then let us continually offer up a sacrifice of praise to God, that is, the fruit of our lips, acknowledging his name. [16] And do not neglect to do good and to share what you have, for God is pleased with such sacrifices.

[17] Obey your leaders and submit to them, for they keep watch over your souls and will give an account for their work. Let them do this with joy and not with complaints, for this would be no advantage for you. [18] Pray for us, for we are sure that we have a clear conscience and desire to conduct ourselves rightly in every respect. [19] I especially ask you to pray that I may be restored to you very soon.

BENEDICTION AND CONCLUSION

[20] Now may the God of peace who by the blood of the eternal covenant brought back from the dead the great shepherd of the sheep, our Lord Jesus, [21] equip you with every good thing to do his will, working in us what is pleasing before him through Jesus Christ, to whom be glory forever. Amen.

[22] Now I urge you, brothers and sisters, bear with my message of exhortation, for in fact I have written to you briefly. [23] You should know that our brother Timothy has been released. If he comes soon, he will be with me when I see you. [24] Greetings to all your leaders and all the saints. Those from Italy send you greetings. [25] Grace be with you all.

RESOURCES

Additional articles, developed by *The Abide Bible* team, are available for free on the Thomas Nelson Bibles website to supplement your Scripture engagement endeavor, to let "the word of Christ dwell in you richly" (Col 3:16).

HOW TO ABIDE IN GOD'S WORD: Learn how to come to the Scriptures in a manner that promotes a thriving, living, transforming relationship with Christ.

5 STEPS TO ENGAGE WITH THE BIBLE: Following these five steps will help you prepare to engage with God's Word so it becomes more personally meaningful and transformative in your life.

CHRIST, THE CENTER OF SCRIPTURE: It is through the Bible that we meet and know Christ. When we grow in our love for Christ, we grow in our love of Scriptures.

HOW IS SCRIPTURE ENGAGEMENT DIFFERENT FROM BIBLE STUDY? Scripture engagement is a complement to deep study of the Scriptures, engaging both the mind and the heart for a deepened relationship with God and a changed life.

SCRIPTURE ENGAGEMENT AND THE SPIRITUAL DISCIPLINES: Spiritual disciplines are means to saturate our lives with the Bible, engaging with it so that our lives are transformed.

HOW NOT TO READ THE BIBLE: God's Word is good and profitable, but there are some ways of approaching the Bible that can end up restricting spiritual growth.

Find these articles and more *Abide Bible Journal* resources
thomasnelsonbibles.com/abide-bible-journals